The Trail of Tears

The 19th Century Forced Migration of Native Americans

D1522486

Table of Contents

Introduction

The Trail of Tears is a fascinating story that revolves around the forced removal of the Native Americans from their ancestral lands in the United States in the 19th century. The tale of Native Americans is one of the most famous genocide anecdotes in world history.

Native Americans are known by various names such as Indigenous Americans, American Indians, and the Indigenous people of the United States (apart from Hawaii). They inhabited the entire region of the American continent and surrounding regions, right from the Arctic point to the tip of the southern American continent. Several tribes settled in one region and distributed parts of their land to live on and cultivate. During their time, they built temples to worship and developed a structured lifestyle pattern. Other tribes or nomads traveled across the flat lands of the continent.

To understand the occurrence and consequences of the Trail of Tears, it is necessary to first learn about the significant parts of the history of Native Americans - where they came from, how they were controlled, and the consequences. It's also important to learn about the European settlers that invaded the Indian land and enforced brutal acts over the tribal people.

This book will cover all aspects related to the removal of the Native Americans from their homelands, in detail. You will also gain an overview of their history, how they settled in their native lands, the role of American leaders in deciding their fate, and how the heinous removal act was later known as the Trail of Tears. The last chapter also provides an insight into the repercussions and the current scenario of the natives. Read on to find out.

Chapter 1:

History of the Native Americans

This chapter covers the entire history of Native Americans - how they settled in their lands, how they grew, and how they were oppressed by the colonizers. It is necessary to understand their history before moving on to the Trail of Tears directly; this is because Native Americans have been marginalized to a great extent. Whether it is geographical or metaphorical, people have forgotten about the Native Americans. Those who know about it connect to their story with a sense of pity or revile.

Also, this group of people formed a small percentage of groups that resisted oppression and fought for their freedom - not once, but multiple times. Moreover, Native Americans also displayed an example of how you could act in historical dominance and not be acted upon.

Native Americans lived in the southern parts of the territory and occupied most of the fertile land for several generations. The name 'Indians' was denoted by Christopher Columbus when he mistakenly believed that he had landed in the Indies. Columbus landed on the American land in 1492, where millions of people belonging to the indigenous tribes inhabited the region. With the advent of 1900, less than 300,000 people survived in the region.

During the later stages of the Ice Age, several inhabitants in Siberia traveled to Alaska through the Bering Land Bridge, which was a stretch of land that connected Siberia to Alaska. This stretch of land was a difficult journey to cover as it was inhabited by several animals, some of which were dangerous. The journey was not limited to only one group. Many groups of varying ethnicities traveled across the stretch and settled around the regions over the next thousands of years. This is proven by the archaeological remains of prints, animal parts related to bison, moose, elk, and mammoth, tools, and evidence of fire pits in the regions. The evidence dates back to 14,500 years ago, which is almost at the end of the Ice Age. It is also known that these people were avid craftsmen who developed specialized tools to hunt big animals for meat and fur.

As time passed, they started moving to the southern parts of the Alaskan region, which eventually led them to Mexico and other parts of the United States. As generations passed, their descendants explored and started settling around the western coast of the United States. By 1000 BC, most of these inhabitants settled in and around the continent of North America. Some of these tribes continuously migrated from one continent to the other for over one thousand years. Due to their constant migration, they developed several languages, cultures, and even civilizations. These native Indian Americans belonged to different tribes and continents, mainly in Asia, Europe, and Africa.

One of the first groups of Native Americans, the Paleo Indians, would often hunt mammoths and mastodons. Next, the Archaic Indians (they survived around the period of 5000 to 1000 BC) would hunt bison or American buffalos in the Colorado plains and be proficient in developing cave art. Slowly and steadily, most of these groups converted into an agricultural society.

As soon as the Ice Age ended, the Native Americans further developed smaller groups or tribes that followed a particular language, culture, and habitat. They used the natural resources that were available to them and developed an agricultural and farming base. They grew crops like squash and corn and tended to farm animals such as Guinea Pigs, llamas, and turkeys for food and other lifestyle requirements. Their protein and meat intake was also fulfilled by hunting animals like deer, sea mammals, bison, and fish. They formulated their own method to hunt and to catch fish.

One extremely interesting development that can be noted with the olden times of the Native Americans in the development of mounds using heaps of sand. These mounds were established in a trail known today as the mid-western parts of the United States to the southern part of Peru. As mentioned, these mounds were built with huge heaps of sand that were flat on the top. They signified an essential part of the tribal government of that era. Buildings such as palaces or temples were built on the top of these mounds. Some mounds were also used to build burial sites of influential leaders. As it suggests, various tribes of Indians had widely spread across the continents.

The American Indians rapidly developed these cities and internal infrastructures. The development was so mind-boggling and impressive that they can be compared to the scale of European cities today. They also paid maximum attention to architecture and city planning, so much so that people still admire their architectural expertise.

When the European invasion took place in the American continent after 1492, the historical and cultural changes were noteworthy. By that year, the Indians had developed a static agrarian culture lifestyle, where they hunted and cultivated to live and eat. The colonization had a significant impact on the differences between the old and new worlds. We know how colonization affected the American continent as it completely changed its historical implication. The Gulf Coast and the regions around Florida were hit first by Spanish invaders; this led to a rapid decline of the Native American population, mostly between the 16th and 19th centuries.

Another reason for the decline was a rising epidemic and diseases that were entirely beyond their control. Since the Europeans brought with them their diseases, the Native Americans did not have competent immunities to fight these diseases, and this caused numerous deaths. Some of these diseases were chickenpox, cholera, measles, yellow fever, and many others. Since these diseases were prevalent in Europe, the Europeans could easily survive through the epidemic.

As the Europeans colonized more areas to benefit from the farmlands for cultivation and to create new jobs for Europeans, they often declared war on the Native Americans to conquer their land.

However, this amalgamation of Europe and America brought several interesting exchanges, which were mostly related to food and commodities. Animals, plants, and insects were constantly exchanged, both knowingly and unknowingly. One such exchange was also known as the 'Columbian Exchange.' Interestingly, though, horses partly managed to escape these exchanges and escape into the wild, eventually leading to an increase in their numbers. The Native Americans then used these horses to conduct day-to-day activities such as carrying goods, traveling, and hunting. Horses were also important during wars and as an entertainment factor during horse races. In addition, American buffalos were another important part of their operations. Buffalos were indigenous to the region and cultured to produce meat. However, this species wasn't the primary source of food for the Native Americans compared to deer and elk.

Native American Lifestyle and Culture

During the period of pre-Colombian America, most of the local people residing in the northern continent of America formed tribes. They built their lives around the natural land and water resources available. On the western coast, most tribes survived through fishing and hunting sea mammals, whereas the natives that occupied plain lands would hunt buffalos and other animals. Most of these tribes would coordinate and form 'leagues' that established peace and unity among all groups. One of the best-known leagues is the Iroquois Confederacy or the Great League of Peace.

Their religion often consisted of ceremonies that celebrated the spiritual world. They would conduct these vibrant celebrations to pray for better yield. As expected, the tribes that depended on hunting asked for more animals, and the agricultural tribes asked for more crops and better harvests. Collectively, most of these groups believed in a single God that was the main creator and the head of all deities. However, they were not as monotheistic as Christians.

Moreover, these tribes also held a differing perception of property compared to the Europeans. Most of the tribal people considered land to be a shared resource that was given out to families for use. However, the families weren't allowed to own their land. They believed that the land, as a resource, was commonly owned by all Native American people. One of their leaders, Blackhawk (a leader of the Sauk tribe), believed that the Great Spirit provided them with abundant land and resources to cultivate and live on. Unless they were cultivating and living upon the land, they had a complete right on the soil. Blackhawk spread this knowledge to other tribes and leaders, which induced a feeling of collective ownership for most of these tribes.

It provokes a general perception of the American Indians as being modest and steering away from greed and class. However, Native Americans were certainly divided into different classes and distinguished according to their lineage and ancestry. For instance, most of the rulers and tribe leaders belonged to the same family or lineage, but money, resources, and overall wealth was evenly distributed among all people. One distinct trait that some of these tribes followed is that children were matrilineal. Even though most of the tribal leaders were men, their children would usually belong to the mother's family. Some of the tribal women converted into religious leaders and often owned tools and dwellings. But since no one had the right to own land, their ownership was limited to dwellings. The ratio of women to men was highly unbalanced. Since there were more women than men, the practice of polygamy was quite common among the tribes - the act of one man marrying several wives to keep the balance.

Among all tribes, the Navajo and the Apache, collectively known as the Athabascan speaking Indians, moved to their homelands before the Europeans invaded their land. Even though these tribes were thought to be in close proximity to each other, their lifestyle habits varied widely. While the Navajo preferred more settled activities, the Apache would usually roam across the lands for hunting animals and to fetch food.

Among the tribe leaders, Geronimo (leader of the Chiricahua group) was a popular figure due to his healing powers.

Colonization by Spanish Settlers

Among all European settlers, the Spanish were the first to invade certain regions of the United States, particularly the ones that were inhabited by Native Americans. In 1513, Juan Ponce de Leone arrived in the southeastern region of the Northern continent, which is now Florida. He wandered around in search of gold, which led him to this region.

Later, in 1521, he was killed by a poison-tipped arrow that was shot by a Calusa brave. Among other Spanish settlers and leaders, another significant name includes Alvar Nunez Cabeza de Vaca (who also explored the southwestern part of the Northern American continent for gold). These Spanish settlers then colonized Florida in anticipation of establishing a military base and defeated the pirates who were eyeing their silver-laden galleons that were located in Mexico. Another reason to colonize the region was to convert the local population to Christianity. The natives did not accept this move and struck back to prevent the missionaries from spreading their Christian beliefs. In 1597, the Guale Indians were the most influential in ruining the missions.

The Spanish colonizers faced many difficulties in colonizing Florida as the weather and lifestyle conditions did not suit their ideal habits. However, they were still successful in colonizing the southwestern part of the continent. Then, in 1610, the European settlers established their first permanent base in a region that is now Santa Fe in New Mexico. The Native Americans were called 'Pueblos' by the Spanish conquerors.

During the Spanish rule, the Native Americans witnessed a major decline in their population and wealth. Between 1600 and 1680, their population reduced from 60,000 to 17,000, which was less than half of their initial population. The Spanish had the upper hand because of the differences in the Native American tribes. The tribal people could not unite and form an alliance to drive away from the Spanish as each tribe had their own thoughts and followed their own ideals.

However, since the Spanish did not leave for many decades, a wise leader known as Pope united the natives and formed an army of 2,000 warriors. Collectively, they murdered 400 Spanish colonizers and drove away the rest from Santa Fe. The natives were successful in tearing down the Spanish establishment in Santa Fe and redeveloping their dwellings and living structure. All Christian buildings and churches were abolished, and kivas (the religious place of the Native Americans) were built in their place. When the Spanish left the Indian region, they left behind their cattle, sheep, and horses. The Indians did not have much use for the horses, which is why they let the animals roam free.

However, with the abundance of animals around them, the Indians faced a substantial cultural change. Within a period of 100 years, the immense horse culture change gave rise to new groups like the Cheyenne, the Camanche, the SU, the Arapaho, and the Kiowa.

In retrospect, the Spanish invaders grew more concerned and tolerated the Indian's religion, and also removed a forced labor practice called encomienda. Among all the brutal Spanish leaders, one of them, whose name was De Las Casas, who witnessed the brutality from his countrymen, turned out to be a noble. The act of cruelty and ignorance that the Spanish invaders showered on the Indians was known as 'The Black Legend.' Most Spanish invaders and leaders believed that the Indians were heathens, and they deserved these horrible repercussions.

Colonization by English Settlers

Now, by 1607, English settlers started invading the regions within the Chesapeake area (now Virginia) that were already inhabited by the Native Americans. The English claimed that they invaded the region to protect the Indians from the brutality of the Spanish, which was not entirely true.

The region was occupied by a few Indian tribes (approximately thirty tribes), who were collectively under the leadership of Chief Wahunsenacawh (the British called him Chief Powhatan for easy pronunciation, which was also the name of his tribe and title). Chief Powhatan was smart and insightful. He instantly realized that the English were beneficial as they had guns. Moreover, the English were clueless about not dying of starvation. Powhatan immediately took this opportunity and decided to help the English in return for gratitude.

The English were so impressed and grateful that colony leader John Smith ordered his colonizer men to arrange for their own food and stop stealing it from the Indians. Since this relationship between the Indian Americans and the British was beneficial for both parties, they continued to interact and thrive collectively in the region. Now, the Chesapeake area lacked money, particularly gold and silver. At this point, the Virginia Company was the only one that made money. To make more money, they had to indulge in trade.

Now, we would think that the intelligent and powerful Europeans would be quick on their feet and clever enough to indulge the Indians into trading with them at a cheaper rate and impose unfair deals. However, that wasn't the case. The tribes agreed to indulge in a fair trade that involved exchanging surplus goods from each end. The British received fur and food, as the Indians had plentiful. In exchange, the Indians received items such as guns, tools, woven cloth, and iron utensils from the British. The trading relations were maintained in the beginning. However, things took a nasty turn. To maintain trade relations, Indians had to hunt more and provide more food for the British, which diverted their attention from agriculture and growing crops. Since the men were away from home hunting, this also resulted in a gender imbalance within their society.

Moreover, the British had their own perception and said in the Indians' land use, which led to further conflict. They regularly instructed and asked the Natives to change their farming ways, which the Indians felt was intruding at one point. The Indians also experienced a change in their traditional way of living, which eventually led them to protest.

In retrospect, the British constructed a fenced border to separate their land from the Indians'. Moreover, they allowed their animals, mainly cattle and pigs, to roam around on the Indian land to eat and destroy their crops. The British continuously requested more and more fur, which imposed a never-ending demand. It was difficult for the Indians to cope, and this led to internal conflict among the Natives. They constantly fought to gain a beneficial hunting ground. At one point, the tribes turned against each other and declared war. They even used the guns that were provided by the British.

Meanwhile, there were other issues that concerned the British's dominance over the Native Americans. Chief Powhatan ordered the capture of colonizer leader John Smith and kept him under observation. This was a major sign for the colonizers to understand Indian dominance. However, Chief Powhatan's daughter, Pocahontas, rescued John Smith, which seemed like a planned move to convey a message to the British colonizers.

It was believed that Pocahontas would marry John Smith, which wasn't true. However, in 1613, she was caught and held captive for ransom. After her release, she married another British man, John Rolfe. Later, she moved to England with Rolfe and converted to Christianity. Due to exposure to a new environment and diseases, her immunity did not protect her, and she died after a few years. During her time in England, she became quite popular and was considered a sensation among the British. The period after Pocahontas' and Rolfe's marriage (mainly around 1614) was comparatively peaceful.

Moving back to John Smith and his invasion of the Indians, he was injured in an explosion of gunpowder, and he returned to England. With this move, the Indians and other British colonizers entered into further conflict. Once John Smith was out of the picture, the British continued their old routine and started stealing food from the Indians and ruining their crops. They even led a massacre, which completely deteriorated the relationship between the Indians and the colonizers.

Later, in 1622, Chief Opechancanough gathered the tribes and decided to attack the British. They feared that this colonization was rapidly increasing, and soon they would be deprived of basic necessities such as food and fur in the name of trade. If this continued, the British would soon take the entire land and capture the Indians. This realization led the Indians to rebel against the British. As expected, the British fought back, and the consequences were dire - the Indians remained under the colonization of the British. This also partly led to the failure of the Virginia Company. During its time, the company was sponsoring around 6,000 colonists, which did not provide any noteworthy profit.

In 1644, the Indians decided to strike again, which was another failed attempt. By this time, only 2,000 Native Americans thrived within the community. These Indians were then urged to sign treaties and move to the west of the Virginian region.

While most of these English colonizers were cruel and unfair to the Indians, there were a few Puritans that tried to be impartial with them. Apart from John Smith, Roger Williams made an effort to offer fair treatment for the Indians. However, most of these British men thought that the Indians did not deserve their land as they weren't treating or using it properly. One such leader, John Winthrop, attempted to take Indian land by buying it instead of seizing it. There was one catch here, though. By selling their land, the Indians had to submit themselves to English authority.

Now, the Purists built an ambiguous opinion of the Indians. On the one hand, they thought that the Indians needed to be rescued and pushed in the direction of well-being. This is also evident from a Massachusetts seal that portrays an Indian saying, "Come over and help us." At the same time, the Purists also felt that the Indians were content with their lives as they had abundant resources, food, land, and shelter. Moreover, women's equality was honored among the tribes, which was quite progressive in that era, and this might have lured some outsiders into wanting to become a part of the Natives.

To protect the people from joining the indigenous life, the Massachusetts General Court ruled out a three-year hard labor sentence prescription in 1642 for those who joined the tribes and lived with them. Summaries of these rulings even became a part of books as anti-Indian propagandas. The scripts declared the desire of the Europeans and the British to return to their Christian lifestyle and leave the tribes - these revolved around captivity tales. In one such book, titled Sovereignty and Goodness of God by Mary Rowlandson, the emphasis was quite contradicting. The book mentioned that the Indians did not bash their European captives and, instead, treated them well.

During this time, Powhatan had proved to be an effective leader for the tribes; at the same time, New England sincerely lacked a powerful leadership. In 1637, the English and the Indian's animosity struck again, which was known as the Pequot War. During this war, a Pequot village at Mystic was burned, and around 500 people were killed. The war was due to the growing desire of the Narragansett Indians, who wanted to take over the Pequots. Additionally, some soldiers from Massachusetts (which was a new colony in Connecticut at the time) joined the war. An English fur trader was also killed by some Pequots. This period was one of the biggest massacres of the time, which continued for several months.

Since the Indians were already low in number from the beginning, they could not match the armies and were defeated; most Indians were killed or sent to the Caribbean as slaves. Furthermore, the war also continued over the Connecticut River, where other settlements were established. Since Indians were already low in number, they could not fight the war. They also lacked the advanced weapons their enemies had. The war was brutal and far worse than what some Purists had anticipated, so much so that William Bradford declared in shock, "It was a fearful sight to see them frying in the fire." Even though the New England natives felt outnumbered, they continued to resist the British.

With the advent of 1675, the remaining Native Americans wanted to fight back and resist New England colonists. This was known to be the biggest war that the Indians launched during that period and was called King Philip's War. Metacom, who was a Wampanoag Chief, led the resistance war, sometimes called Metacom's War. On the contrary, the British referred to Metacom as King Philip due to cultural sensitivity, which is why it was also known as King Philip's war. The Natives emerged as brave warriors, and the consequences were extremely brutal. The resistance, which was over the course of two years, was partly successful as major English settlements were ripped apart in the northeastern region. There were around ninety English towns that were established in the Indian settlements, and the Indians attacked more than half and destroyed about twelve of those settlements.

Around 52,000 European colonizers and 20,000 Indian Americans were involved in this war. Among these, 1,000 Europeans and 3,000 Indians died. Among other battles, the Battle of the Great Swamp destroyed the population of the Indians by a massive number. In King Philip's War, the leader was killed, and his head was placed in the Plymouth Town Square for a couple of decades.

Nathaniel Saltonstall, a witness, said, "The heathen rarely gave quarter to those that they take, but if they were women, the first forced them to satisfy their filthy lusts and then murdered them." Furthermore, Saltonstall also observed how the Natives killed the colonists' cows and described it as, "Cutting their bellies and letting them go several days trailing their guts after them," which seems like a horrendous scenario. The reason why the Indians attacked the enemies' cattle and livestock indicated a rising fear among them; they believed that the grazing pattern of the colonists' livestock was steadily increasing their territorial rule, which would soon suppress their lifestyle. These were some signs of brutality portrayed by the Indians that declared their rage against New England settlers. Another remorseless act that enraged the symbolism of this war involved the Indians' disembowelment toward a colonist and placing a Bible in his body cavity.

It showed that the Indians had enough of the colonist's heinous acts, and they would no longer suffer by fighting for their rights and lands. All in all, the Puritans wanted to expand their Christian territory over the world, and only after fifty years of its founding. Their final goal, however, seemed to be a failure (at least for the time being). It was also believed that if they were entirely right and they wouldn't face such a big massacre and brutal act of force from the Indians where they burned their houses and were murdered. They considered it to be a sign from God.

Chapter 2:

Issues with the Native Americans

After the United States of America was proclaimed as an independent nation post-American Revolution in the middle of the 18th century, the country fought against the British to garner power over the Native American regions that were established in the eastern part of the Mississippi River. Foreseeing some gruesome consequences, the Native Americans joined and sided with the British. The natives were also involved in trading influences with the British. Moreover, they hoped to decrease the chances of further colonial expansion that was steadily rising. The United States had a major goal of expanding their lands, settlements, and farming areas for their growing populations. The new immigrants and settlers from New England were also eager to get new land and opportunities for their population.

When the United States was forming into an independent nation, a parallel event occurred that formed a new Indian culture, also known as the Warrior Horse culture. The occurrence of these two events would end in a massive clash due to rising differences. The Plains Indian horse culture was an honest warrior society that had immensely evolved over the past 50 to 100 years. They were thoroughly prepared to protect their land and fight for their lives.

The conflict between the United States of America and the Native Americans can be dated back to 1837 when Martin Van Buren was in power and seated in the White House. The trail of Santa Fe experienced a busy routine of traders that constantly traveled to and fro. Another trail was the Oregon path that transferred some settlers.

The father of the U.S. Cavalry, Stephen Watts Kerning, wrote and produced a manual for the United States dragoons who acted as the frontrunners and represented the country's top-notch cavalry soldiers. They were provided with high-quality uniforms and superior weapons.

The United States government saw this as a rising opportunity to spur growth by seizing the land of the Native Americans, either by peaceful means or by forced exile.

Chapter 3:

Role of American Leaders

American leaders played a major role in deciding the fate of the American Indians. All leaders that were a part of the Revolutionary and Early National period had constant discussions and debates regarding the national identity of the Native Americans. They constantly tended to a rising question - should the American Indians become a part of the nation, or should they be given a separate identity?

Benjamin Franklin

On May 10, 1775, Benjamin Franklin proposed a draft known as the 'Proposed Articles of Confederation' to the Continental Congress. He suggested that a 'perpetual Alliance' should be encouraged between the Native Americans and the United States as it was about to witness its transformation with the Six Nations of the Iroquois Confederacy. According to his proposed declaration, Benjamin

Franklin said that the Native Americans would not be disturbed or asked to be evacuated from their lands. Moreover, he also mentioned that their lands should not be encroached on or colonized by the country. There would be no deals between the General Congress and the Great Council of the Indians at Onondaga for any form of land reforms or purchase. Basically, the draft looked toward the protection of the Indian Americans and their borders; it made sure that they did not face any injustice.

Thomas Jefferson

Next in line was Thomas Jefferson. In 1785, Thomas Jefferson sided with the Native Americans and declared his amazement toward the tribes. In the 'Notes on the State of Virginia,' he mentioned that the Native Americans had, "A moral sense of right and wrong," and they "never submitted themselves to any laws, any coercive power, any shadow of government." Later, in 1785, he mentioned in the Marquis de Chastellux, "I believe the Indian then to be in body and mind equal to the white man." As Francis Paul Prucha interpreted from his writings, his main purpose was to mingle both the worlds

(Native Americans and European Americans) and encourage them to thrive as a single community with peace and harmony. To do that, he was even willing to offer U.S. citizenship to the Native Americans and indulge them to increase their trading relations by offering credit.

When Thomas Jefferson was in power, he designed a policy that aimed at fulfilling two objectives:

1. He wanted the Native nations to be connected to the United States operations; this was to ensure the security of the newly-found nation.

2. He wanted the Native Americans to adopt a better lifestyle. Instead of living as hunters, he wanted the tribal people to turn toward agriculture and become more civilized.

He subtly included these objectives within the trading policies and designed treaties. To meet his desire to civilize the tribes, he often expressed his wish of uniting the white settlers with the natives and living in a unified and diverse nation. This is evident in one of his letters written on November 3,

1802, and addressed to the Seneca spiritual leader, which said,

"Go on then, brother, in the great reformation you have undertaken.... In all your enterprises for the good of your people, you may count with confidence on the aid and protection of the United States, and on the sincerity and zeal with which I am myself animated in the furthering of this humane work. You are our brethren of the same land; we wish your prosperity as brethren should do. Farewell."

Source: https://en.m.wikipedia.org/wiki/Indian_removal

After his continuous efforts, one of the influential members from the Cherokee nation expressed the group's desire to acquire citizenship and become a formal part of the nation, as previously promised by George Washington (read on to understand his role).

Thomas Jefferson agreed to accommodate and offer citizenship. On November 8, 1808, he offered a similar response in his Eighth Annual Message to Congress. He expressed how the Indians and the white settlers could peacefully thrive in society and grow together. He also felt that the white settlers needed to offer a hand of friendship as the Indian population was rapidly gaining strength. The Cherokee nation had two divisions, out of which had gained Jefferson's word to gain citizenship.

On the contrary, some of his writings depicted his ambivalent nature toward Indian assimilation. He used words such as 'extirpate' and 'exterminate,' which showed his growing fear toward the Indians. He believed that the tribes could go against the Americans to gain their rights and power, which would be a damaging impact on American development.

There was also a hidden sentiment behind designing his policies. By switching to agriculture instead of hunting, Jefferson assumed that the Native Americans would turn to white settlers for trading influences. They would then have to be dependent on the white people to buy goods in order to survive. This would, ultimately, oblige them to give up their lands to the Americans. If not, they would be urged to move to the other region of the Mississippi River. In 1803, Jefferson also wrote a private letter to William Henry Harrison, in which he mentioned his real objectives. He said that if any tribal group failed to follow the desired path, they would be urged to give up their land and move to another region. He believed that this move would also serve as a great example to others who would not cooperate.

At the same time, his letter also mentioned the actual concern he had for Indians. He mentioned how his system would be operating toward maintaining a peaceful relationship with the Indians and considering their needs. He wished that the white people would live in harmony and practice justice.

According to the treaty of February 27, 1819, the U.S. government declared that the Cherokee nation that was particularly settled in the eastern region of the Mississippi River was to receive citizenship along with 640 acres of land for each family.

So, in simple words, the Jefferson policy indicated that the land exchange between the United States and Native Americans would take place based on trading relationships and a change in the Indian lifestyle. In case of failure, the Indians would be giving away their lands on the western part of the Mississippi River for a smaller region in the eastern part. This idea was initiated by Thomas Jefferson, which was tweaked and mentioned in the Indian Removal Act with harsher implications.

George Washington

George Washington was another important part of the Native American tale. In 1790, the President, in his declaration to the Seneca nation, said that the pre-Constitutional Indian land sale was unjust and did not protect the rights of the natives. He took further steps by personally meeting fifty tribal chiefs in Philadelphia; this also included the Iroquois. He suggested ways to keep both the tribes and the white settlers united. He also emphasized the importance and need to keep peace with the natives in his Fourth Annual Message to Congress. In his message, he also mentioned the need for qualified people to reside among the natives as agents. This would establish not only a peaceful relationship between both parties but also ensure the regulation of the government's actions. George Washington also wanted to keep a trading relationship with the Native Americans and promote civilization.

Later, he again emphasized the growing need to improve their relationship with the Indians. In his Seventh Annual Message to Congress, he said that it was a give and take relationship. If the United States wanted the raid to stop, they would have to stop it too. They would achieve peace only if they agreed to give peace.

Chapter 4:

The Indian Removal Act

The constant conflict between the white settlers and Native American Indians was going to cause a trifling removal act that could cause thousands of deaths and imprisonment.

John C. Calhoun's Plan

The Secretary of War under President James Monroe, John C. Calhoun was the first authority to design the removal act that could lead to tens of thousands of Native Americans losing their land and homes from the regions around the Mississippi River. After a while, at the end of 1824, James Monroe agreed to pass Calhoun's proposal. On January 27, 1825, his message to the Senate informed the formation of the Arkansas Territory and Indian Territory. With this formation, the Native Americans had to exchange their eastern lands for the western regions of the Mississippi River. The Senate had a decisive say about this decision and ordered Calhoun to draft a relevant bill.

However, the Georgia delegation in the House of Representatives did not pass the bill. When John Quincy Adams was in charge as the President, he considered the same policy designed by Calhoun and Monroe, but he wanted the Indians to move without being forced upon. However, the state of Georgia did not agree to this policy and forced Adams to convince the Cherokees to sign a treaty that gave Georgia the rights to Cherokee lands. In contrast, the Cherokee nation also devised a constitution on July 26, 1827, that declared the Cherokee as an independent nation, and they operated on their own means.

Georgia resisted this move and declared their disapproval to countenance a sovereign state within their region.

Andrew Jackson and His Policy Design

Between the period between 1820 and 1850, many government policies changed. More people were allowed to vote, state legislatures diminished massively, and some were even eliminated. However, though, there was a catch here. These changes were only applicable if you were white and a male. By the time Andrew Jackson was elected as the president of the United States in 1829, most of the states had discarded their property rights, except for North Carolina, Rhode Island, and Virginia. This is a significant reason why he got elected.

During this time, the American System that was developed was based on economic nationalism. Two of the main supporters of this American System included Henry Clay and John C. Calhoun, who were also Jeffersonian Republicans. They were supposed to be in that party, as it was the only political party of the time. The laws within the American System mostly consisted of federally financed internal improvements (relating to infrastructures such as roads and canals), capital and tariffs to construct and support new factories, and the development of a new national bank that was supposed to replace the first bank of the United States. This era was collectively known as the 'Era of Good Feelings.'

The rapid changes within the American territories gave way to further development and greed for ownership. The leaders believed that by gaining power over more land, they could enhance development and provide an optimum settlement for their citizens.

Andrew Jackson, who belonged to Tennessee, was an important name in the removal act of the Native Americans. In 1830, he signed a petition known as the Indian Removal Act that indicated the removal of the Native Americans from their regions and shelter in Georgia, North Carolina, Alabama, Florida, and Tennessee. They were forced to relocate to another region that was deemed as the 'Indian Territory,' which is now recognized as Oklahoma. The federal government wanted power over the eastern region of Mississippi that was crowded by the Native American tribes.

It was not until Andrew Jackson came into the picture that the Removal Act became an official U.S. policy. Even before he became the president, he was majorly involved in the process of winning the conflict over the Native Americans. Andrew Jackson's view over the Indian Removal Act was completely contradicting to his predecessors. Unlike most former presidents who wanted to collaborate with the

Native Americans peacefully, Andrew Jackson took a different path. He always believed that the government could take the land from the Indians solely through forced exile. He made sure that the Indians who claimed constitutional sovereignty and voluntarily freed themselves from the state laws underwent dreadful and aggressive repercussions.

He led the War of 1812, where he instructed the clearing of the regions surrounding the Mississippi River for the white settlement to control. Followed by this was his participation in the First Seminole War, led under the presidency of James Monroe, which evacuated the Seminole tribe of Florida.

Furthermore, the white settlers in and around Georgia constantly complained about 'wishing' to inhabit the region that was inhabited by the Native Americans. During this time, Andrew Jackson was yet to enter the White House, but he always kept records of the complaints and issues that white settlers faced. One of the main complaints, among many others, involved the settlement of the Cherokee and Creek people in Georgia.

In 1828, white settlers in Georgia felt confident after the election of Andrew Jackson, which naturally led to the cancelation of the constitution of the Cherokee nation and stating that the Indians in Georgia were subjected to and obliged to follow the state laws. When Andrew Jackson was in power during his second term, he constantly pressurized Congress to rule the bill and give official permission to eradicate the Native Americans from their regions.

However, in 1830, the Cherokee nation decided to fight back and took the case to the Supreme Court. They wanted the state of Georgia to be declared as a free nation and not subjected to the laws of the state as an authority. To their surprise, Chief Justice of the Supreme Court, John Marshall declared that the Cherokee nation would be deemed as a distinct society and not a distinct nation.

John Marshall also declared that the state of Georgia did not have authority over the Cherokee Nation. But the Cherokee nation was still subject to the federal government as it was a sovereign nation; this move induced a feeling of acting as sovereign nations among the tribes and the federal government. When President Andrew Jackson came into power, he commanded the removal of the Native

Americans by designing and signing the Indian Removal Act of 1830. This act declared the voluntary removal of the natives to the west of the Mississippi River. However, due to lack of cooperation, the Indians were forcibly removed, some of whom were killed and some imprisoned. Congress saw to it that the Native Indians were entirely eradicated from the area, which led to the development of the Bureau of Indian Affairs.

While Andrew Jackson was keen on implementing this act, not all leaders or official representatives of the government-supported this act. One such contradicting leader was Tennessee Rep. Davy Crockett, who vocally expressed his disgruntlement regarding the country's immoral actions.

Chapter 5:

The Trail of Tears

The name 'Trail of Tears' is based on the horrendous act of forcibly removing and killing Native Americans by the federal government. Tens of thousands of natives fled their homes in terror. The Indian Removal Act was majorly inclined toward the removal of the 'Five Civilized Tribes—Choctaw, Chickasaw, Cherokee, Creek, and Seminole.' These names were formulated by their own people as some of these were exposed to white European culture.

This is how each tribal group suffered after the implication of the Indian Removal Act:

Choctaws

Some of these tribes voluntarily agreed to relocate to other parts while others rebelled and refused to move. The first tribe to sign the treaty, also known as the Treaty of Dancing Rabbit

Creek and relocate to another region, were the Choctaws. They signed the treaty in September 1830 and moved to a region that is now the state of Arkansas; this was one of the biggest Indian moves after the policy was instituted. This move was beneficial for the Choctaws only in the sense of not losing their major population and resettling in peaceful conduct. However, by signing the treaty, the Choctaws gave way to one of the largest regions in the eastern parts of Mississippi for white and European settlers. The Choctaws battled through their journey to settle in another region by going through one of the most dreadful experiences of their lives. When they reached Little Rock, the Chief of Choctaws denoted their path as a "trail of tears and death."

Their devastating experience was also witnessed by a French historian and political thinker named Alexis de Tocqueville in 1831. During his journey, he witnessed a couple of Choctaw men, women, and children near the region of Memphis, Tennessee, who were ready to get on a boat and sail toward their new home in the eastern region of Mississippi River.

In one of his writings, he describes the heart-breaking scene as:

"In the whole scene, there was an air of ruin and destruction, something which betrayed a final and irrevocable adieu; one couldn't watch without feeling one's heart wrung. The Indians were tranquil but somber and taciturn. There was one who could speak English, and of whom I asked why the Chactas were leaving their country. "To be free," he answered, could never get any other reason out of him. We ... watch the expulsion ... of one of the most celebrated and ancient American peoples."

Source: https://en.m.wikipedia.org/wiki/Indian_removal

Seminoles

As we know, the region of Florida was acquired by Spain, after which the U.S. overtook by signing the Adams–Onís Treaty. By 1821, the U.S. acquired the entire possession over Florida, making it an official part and state of the United States of America.

The tribe of Seminoles was settled in Florida (mainly in the Everglades). They were asked to move to the west after being called for a meeting at Payne's Landing on the Ocklawaha River, on the condition that they found the land to be suitable. They were also asked to move in with the Creeks and become an official part of their tribe. However, the Creeks did not allow the Seminoles to be a part of their tribe as they considered the Seminoles to be deserters. The Seminoles were not allowed to be a part of most tribes. Another reason was that some of the existing members of the tribe had converted to Seminoles from Creeks. If they had to move to the western region, they were calling unquestionable death upon themselves. Most of the Creeks were furious about the conversion to Seminoles, which would undeniably spark a dispute.

The job of inspecting the new land and convincing the tribe people to move fell upon the seven appointed chiefs. They did not leave there until October 1832, and after they had conducted a thorough inspection of the new western region and agreed with the already-settled Creek people, they signed the statement that claimed the new land to be acceptable in March 1833. But, when they returned to Florida, some chiefs claimed that they did not sign the statement, whereas the others claimed that they were forced to sign. Either way, they claimed that they did not hold power to make a decision for all people that concerned the reservations. However, in 1834, it was easier for the leaders to persuade the people residing around the Apalachicola River and make a move to the western region.

As expected, the others resisted and refused to leave. They claimed that their land was deeply-rooted in their ancestry and culture. Their refusal and disagreement sparked several surprise attacks on the U.S. Army, one of which was popularly known as the Dade Massacre on December 28, 1835. The war was led by Seminole Chief Osceola, who, along with his army, marched from Fort Brooke in Tampa to Fort King in Ocala. The United States Army faced harsh repercussions after this war. Out of 110 men, only three survived in the U.S. troops. Osceola and his army planned several surprise attacks on the United States Army, most of which were successful. As soon as the U.S. Army began to realize the intensity of their resistance, they too started preparing for the upcoming wars.

The St. Augustine Militia instantly requested 500 muskets on loan from the War Department. Brig. Gen. Richard K. Call additionally organized a troop of 500 men with whom he formulated their attack plan. On the Indian side, families and non-participants fled to other regions or hid in forts; they even raided farms. In another attack led by Osceola (also known as the Second Seminole War), more men were killed and injured. The Atlantic coast, located south of St. Augustine, housed several sugar plantations, which were vastly destroyed. Since the plantation slaves were enraged and wanted to claim vengeance, they joined the Seminole tribe. Apart from these main wars, several attacks took place, which was led by other chiefs of the Seminole tribe such as Halleck Tustenuggee, Black Seminoles Abraham and John Horse, and Jumper.

Collectively, the war ended in 1842. The United States Army lost about 1500 men, about $20 million, which is estimated to be around $529,862,069 today, and vast, valuable resources. However, the United States eventually won and moved the remaining Seminoles to the west of the Mississippi

River. That region was later known as the Indian Territory.

During one of the many fights in 1837, tribe leader Osceola was captured by the United States Army on the orders of U.S. General Thomas Jesup. In order to save his life, Osceola agreed to enter a truce near Fort Peyton. While Seminole chief Osceola was captured by the United States troops, some of the Seminoles managed to stay in Florida. Osceola died in the prison cell due to illness. A few of their descendants can still be found in the region today after some of their ancestors escaped deeper into the Everglades of Florida. Other Seminoles escaped to the western region of the United States. In the end, the government let the remaining Seminoles settle in Florida, which was a group of around 500 people.

As a result, the Seminole tribe in Florida is the only federally recognized tribe that did not enter into an agreement with the United States Army and did not sign any peace treaty. On January 26, 1836, the Virginia Enquirer published an article that was called the 'Hostilities of the Seminoles,' which claimed that the results and difficult repercussions were only because of the Seminoles themselves. They blamed the Indians for their harsh circumstances because of not staying true to their word and not obliging to the Indian Removal Act.

Cherokees

The Cherokees were deemed as the most assimilated among the other tribes. They also considered the option of adapting the culture of the white man to save their lands. By adopting this move, they also hoped to avoid conflict. With this decision, Christian missionaries thrived within the Cherokee tribe for approximately thirty years. During this phase, Cherokee children were sent to schools to learn and speak English. They changed their habits and culture; they even dressed and built houses like a typical white man of that era. They went to the extent to publish their newspapers and a new constitution in the English language. However, these attempts weren't appreciated for long. As soon as the United States officials found gold on their land, their territorial borders and treaty rights were no longer considered.

In 1838, President Martin Van Buren ordered the Cherokees to relocate. The order was sent to General Winfield Scott. While 2,000 Cherokees voluntarily agreed to relocate, around 4,000 died while encountering their trip to present-day Oklahoma. These were referred to as 'the place where they cried' (nu na da ul tsun yi, in Cherokee language) and 'the trail where they cried' (nu na hi du na tlo hi lu i).

The state of Georgia drew out orders for the Natives to leave their land. The Cherokees, in turn, sued to remain on their land. A small group of the Cherokees had an internal discussion and agreed to sign the treaty with the United States on December 29, 1835, which was known to be the Treaty of New Echota. However, the group did not represent the tribe's leadership, and this triggered the rest of the tribe, and they refused to leave. Eventually, they were forced to leave the region and settle in the Indian Territory with other tribes. The Cherokee tribe comprised of approximately 17,000 individuals, out of which 4,000 to 8,000 perished on the Trail of Tears. This was majorly blamed on the small group of voluntary tribal representatives that took the step without the leader's consent.

A noble Missionary organizer, Jeremiah Evarts, encouraged the Indians to fight for their rights and take the issue to the United States Supreme Court. After Georgia vs. Cherokee case was looked into by the Supreme Court, there was another case surrounding Christian missionary, Samuel Worcester. He claimed that the state of Georgia had no right over their distinct community, and as we saw in the previous chapter, Chief Justice John Marshall ruled that the states had no say or authority over these communities. The tribes were only solely answerable to the federal government. Andrew Jackson, as the Chief Executive of the time, had the responsibility of implementing and enforcing the court's ruling. However, he indicated that since John Marshall had ruled out the decision, it was his duty to enforce it as well.

Andrew Jackson also feared the beginning of a civil war between the state militia and federal troops, which obliged him not to enforce Cherokee claims. Jackson was already involved in a tensed nullification crisis with South Carolina, and he did not want to intensify the situation any further. He then preferred to evacuate the Cherokees than to undergo a civil war.

One ruling sided with the Cherokees to establish a peaceful presence. If white settlers wanted to live on the Indian Territory, they needed a license from the state. This was mainly to remove the desires of white missionaries who stood against the removal of Indians.

Furthermore, when Martin Van Buren was elected as the president, he commanded the removal of the Cherokees from Georgia. Additionally, General Winfield Scott led 7,000 soldiers to round up the Cherokees in 1838 and move them to Cleveland in Tennessee. The treaty was imposed by Martin Van Buren but was signed by Andrew Jackson.

It also lured many illegal settlers to occupy the Cherokee lands in Georgia due to the increasing population and bright farming opportunities. The situation also intensified when gold was discovered in Cherokee land. In 1829, in a region near Dahlonega in Georgia, a massive amount of gold was discovered, which resulted in the 'Georgia Gold Rush.'

During their journey on the Trail of Tears, the Cherokees faced many difficulties, which resulted in several deaths. It was either because of harsh weather, malnutrition, or disease. The group initiated their journey from Red Clay in Tennessee at the end of 1838. They lacked proper clothing and conducted the journey on foot, without any shoes. Also, the Cherokees weren't allowed to pass through many villages and regions in fear of spreading diseases, which elongated their journey. On December 3, 1838, they reached the Ohio River after covering the regions of Tennessee and Kentucky. In order to cross the river on Berry's Ferry, every Cherokee Indian was charged $1 ($24 value today), which was way more than the usual 12 cents ($3 today) that were charged per head. They were also forced to take shelter under Mantel Rock. Some Cherokees died at the spot, some were killed by locals, and a few others died on the way. The others wanted to bury the dead Cherokees, for which they sued the U.S. government through the courthouse in Vienna, demanding $35 each ($840 today).

Their journey from Ohio to Mississippi River took around three months. The Cherokees that decided to leave in the beginning voluntarily had already figured a water path that took them through Tennessee, Mississippi, and Ohio Rivers within twenty-one days. The forced Cherokees decided to settle in the regions around Tahlequah in Oklahoma. Around 100 Cherokees fled during the war and resided in the neighboring parts of Georgia and other states. Some of them established individual identities and lived on privately-owned lands; by doing so, they were allowed to stay. For instance, there was a group of about 400 Cherokees (also known as the Oconaluftee Cherokees) - they lived in the area of the Great Smoky Mountains in North Carolina, which was owned by William Holland Thomas. Because of this, they were allowed to stay. In the same manner, the Cherokees from the Nantahala region, which then resettled in the Qualla Border, were allowed to stay because of their assistance in finding Tlasi's family. They were then famously known as the Eastern Band of the Cherokee Nation.

Even though many died during the journey, the population of Cherokees eventually sprung back, and they are now the largest group of surviving Indians in the United States of America.

Creeks (Muskogee)

After the Battle of Horseshoe Bend in the War of 1812 that involved the Creeks and the United States, the former was forced to give up their ancestral lands, which covered over 20,000 acres in the Treaty of Fort Jackson. The tribe leader William McIntosh signed the treaty that relinquished a significant chunk of their land to Georgia. The rest of the Creek tribe then voluntarily agreed to sign and give up their lands to the United States. The Treaty of Fort Jackson and the Treaty of Washington repercussions led the Creeks to settle in a region that is now recognized as east-central Alabama. Tribe leaders Big Warrior and Selocta communicated their desire to keep peace with Andrew Jackson. At the time of signing the treaty, Selocta also made an effort to reduce the government's demand for the Creek lands.

Later, in 1825, the Creeks entered into another treaty with the government on February 12, which was known as the Treaty of Indian

Springs. By this point, the Creeks had to give up their remaining lands to Georgia. After the treaty was signed by the tribe leaders and affirmed by the U.S. Senate, Chief William McIntosh was killed by the Creeks after following the orders of Menawa, on April 30, 1825.

However, Opothle Yohola, the leader of the Creek National Council, claimed that the Treaty of Indian Springs was unfair, unjust, and fraudulent. President John Quincy Adams heard their plea and agreed to nullify the treaty by passing a new order that was known as the Treaty of Washington, 1826. Many historians of the time praised the Creeks' efforts by saying that the tribe achieved and received a contracting agreement in their favor, which no other tribe was successful in doing. However, Georgia was still not in their favor and desired to get all their land. This led Governor Troup of Georgia to push the Creeks out of their territory and forcibly exile them. They made this move by following the orders of the first treaty. President Adams made an attempt to control this situation by talking to the federal troops. However, President Adams had to give up in fear of conceding a civil war eventually.

He considered the Indians not to be "worthy enough" to wage war over.

In one of his final addresses to the Creeks in 1829, Andrew Jackson expressed his concern for the Native Americans. He claimed that he was always honest with the Indians and that he "loved his white and red children equally." He also expressed how the white people and Indians could not thrive in harmony because of their close proximity. Since America was a vast land, he urged the Indians to move to the other part of the territory, where the whites wouldn't disturb them. While they can live there and raise their families, the whites will have no claim over their lands, and they could live there "as long as the grass grows or the water runs, in peace and plenty." Moreover, he also claimed that the country would provide for the stock losses and necessary improvements in the new territory.

By 1837, almost 15,000 Creeks reached Fort Gibson that was located within the Indian Territory. Among the 15,000 individuals, around 3,000 died due to harsh weather and starvation. They then moved to the west of the Mississippi River, too, and settled in the Indian Territory. The Lower

Creeks settled in the Indian Territory, and around 20,000 Upper Creeks settled in Alabama. The Indians were forced to follow and obey state laws and were refused their right to function as independent nations. On March 24, 1832, another treaty was ruled out, which was known as the Treaty of Cusseta. According to this treaty, the lands of the Creeks were divided into individual groups and allotments. Now, the Creeks had two choices. They could either sell their allotments and move to the west, or alternatively stay in Alabama and follow the state's laws.

In a collective sense, the Creeks could never achieve a fair agreement. Many Americans would illegally establish their properties on Creek lands, and the federal government did not do enough to stop these fraudulent and unjust acts. Some Creeks, out of rage, consistently raided the region's farms and conducted other crimes to express their anger. It eventually led to several open wars between the United States government and the Indians. In May 1836, one such war caused major damage to the village of Roanoke that is located in Georgia alongside the Chattahoochee River.

Later, in 1835 and 1836, the remaining Indians were forced to move the western region of the Mississippi River. They took a path toward Oklahoma, which was one of the deadliest experiences of their lives. These parts that marked their journey and the regions in which they were about to settle (also known as the Indian Territory) were collectively known as the Trail of Tears, which was a 2200-mile journey. The name, Trail of Tears, is mainly because several natives died during their journey, either due to forced exile or because of starvation, harsh weather, and disease. They lacked shoes and clothes. The food provided by the United States government was mostly rotten or bad.

As per recent findings by historian Billy Winn, many drafts were designed to remove the Creeks from their allotments, which also included representatives from outside of Alabama, Georgia, and Columbus.

Chiricahuas

One such tribe, the Chiricahua Apache, was expatriated from their region and sent to Arizona. Once again, in 1876, they were forced to relocate to another region toward the West. In an attempt to save their tribe, leader Geronimo led some of his people to Mexico and others to participate in raids in the Arizona region. The conflict between the federal government and the Chiricahuas went on for years, which eventually resulted in the Chiricahuas surrendering in 1885. The army of the United States decided to detain them for two years, which the Chiricahuas agreed to. The detention agreement wasn't fully implemented by the United States Army, and they sent many natives to prisons, some of which were located far from their homes. Many of them were held captive as prisoners of wars, without trial, for up to twenty-seven years.

Many tribes followed the path and instructions of the Chiricahua Apache, which took a wrong turn. Their resistance toward the white settlers and the military was brave but in vain as most of the natives were either killed or imprisoned.

Chickasaws

Another group, the Chickasaws, decided to leave without causing a war. However, they demanded a $3 million settlement to leave their region, quite contrary to the other groups' land exchange demands and settlements. The Chickasaws received a sum of $530,000 after agreeing to exchange the land that was previously owned by the Choctaws. However, this took five years and several debates before the Chickasaws received any amount. The amount received was paid for the westernmost part of Choctaw land. The United States initially refused to pay the $3 million but eventually paid them thirty years later. Most of the Chickasaws migrated in the new region between the period of 1837 and 1838.

Among all groups, the first group of Chickasaw to move into the Indian Territory was led by John M. Millard in 1836. On July 4, 1836, he ordered the group members to gather at Memphis with all their belongings, including their cattle, stock, and slaves. They took the same route as the Choctaws and the Creeks, which assisted them in easily and quickly navigating their route. When they reached the Indian Territory, they requested the Choctaw nation to let them be a part of their tribe.

Other Tribes (Based on Location)

While the above mentioned five tribes were the main groups that faced the removal issues, there were several other tribes in the northern and southern regions of the United States that faced harsh circumstances.

Northern Region

The main tribes in the Old Northwestern regions consisted of Shawnee, Ottawa, Potawatomi, Sauk, and Meskwaki (Fox). Since these groups were smaller and widely scattered across the northern region, the evacuation process took more time. However, most of these groups agreed to the treaty policies and signed them without much hesitation. One group, which is Sauk, got involved in a war with the U.S. military. Since the war was led by their chief named Black Hawk, it was widely known as the Black Hawk War. However, the Illinois militia, along with the U.S. Army, defeated Black Hawk and his Sauk and Fox band, which resulted in their migration to a region that is now recognized as Iowa.

Eastern Region

The eastern region accommodated the Lenape (or Delaware tribe), along with the Kickapoo and Shawnee. With the onset of the 1820s, they were exiled from the regions of Michigan, Ohio, and Indiana. Also, the Potawatomi were moved to the Kansas region in 1838. Moreover, the groups that were settled in present-day Ohio were moved to the region of Louisiana. Two years later, in 1840, another group joined the already-settled tribes in the Indian Territory, which was the Miami.

In 1838, the Senecas signed the Second Treaty of Buffalo Creek, which indicated the exchange of the Indian New York land for 200,000 acres of land in the Indian Territory. After the treaty was ruled out, the U.S. government ended up selling all of the acquired lands and added the money to the U.S. Treasury. With this move, the Senecas felt betrayed and decided to take it to the U.S. Court of Claims. The case, however, continued for a while and finally arrived at a verdict in 1898. The U.S. government was obliged to pay $1,998,714.46 to the Indians that owned the New York lands.

In the past, the U.S. government entered into a treaty with both the Senecas and the Tonawanda Senecas in 1842 and 1857, respectively. The Tonawanda Senecas agreed to give away their land in the western region of the Mississippi River to purchase land from the Ogden Land Company, which they claimed to be their rightful reservation. After about a 100 years later, the Senecas decided to build the Seneca Buffalo Creek Casino, for which they purchased a plot in downtown Buffalo, which measured around nine acres; this plot was a part of their original reservation.

Southern Region

As mentioned, the Southern region witnessed the removal of a massive group of Indians, which formed the five main tribes, namely the Creeks, Choctaws, Chickasaws, Cherokees, and Seminoles.

Here is a tabular representation of the removal figures in rounded numbers.

Nation	Population east of the Mississippi before removal treaty	Removal treaty & year signed	Years of major emigration	Total number emigrated or forcibly removed	Number stayed in Southeast	Deaths during removal	Deaths from warfare
Choctaw	19,554 + white citizens of the Choctaw Nation + 500 black slaves	Dancing Rabbit Creek (1830)	1831–1836	12,500	7,000	2,000–4,000+ (Cholera)	None
Creek	22,700 + 900 black slaves	Cusseta (1832)	1834–1837	19,600	100s	3,500 (disease after removal)	? (Second Creek War)
Chickasaw	4,914 + 1,156 black slaves	Pontotoc Creek (1832)	1837–1847	over 4,000	100s	500–800	None
Cherokee	21,500 + 2,000 black slaves	New Echota (1835)	1836–1838	20,000 + 2,000 slaves	1,000	2,000–8,000	None
Seminole	5,000 + fugitive slaves	Payne's Landing (1832)	1832–1842	2,833	250 500		700 (Second Seminole War)

Source: https://en.m.wikipedia.org/wiki/Indian_removal

Final Settlement

The Native Americans were mainly settled in the present-day Oklahoma region. The northeast corner of the region was mostly occupied by the Cherokees, along with a small patch of land surrounding Kansas. The tribes that resisted and did not make the massive move formed smaller groups within their regions. These included the Eastern Band of Cherokee in North Carolina, the Seminole Tribe of Florida, Creeks in Alabama (also the Poarch Band), and the Mississippi Band of Choctaw Indians.

This map shows the travel route of each group after the forced exile.

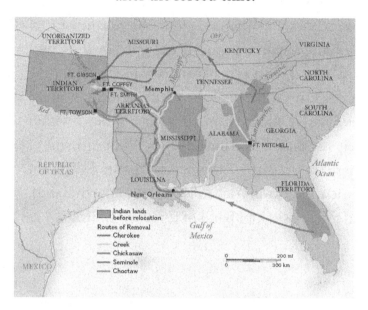

Image source: https://www.nationalgeographic.org/ photo/indian-removal/

Chapter 6:

Repercussions and Current Scenario

With the resettlement of the Native Americans in their new lands, the white settlers were presented with plentiful fertile and lucrative land, majorly in the states of Georgia, Florida, North Carolina, Tennessee, Alabama, Mississippi, and Arkansas.

In today's world, the Trail of Tears is deemed as one of the most important historical chronicles of the United States. It stretches from Tennessee to Oklahoma and specifically mentions the removal of the Cherokee in 1838 and 1839, which was the largest affected tribe group in this act.

Most of the historians and ordinary people that read or evaluate the Indian Removal Act and its repercussions deem this act as harsh, unfair, and unacceptable. The acceptance by the general populace in order to benefit from the concept of Manifest destiny furthered the severity of the situation. Several harsh terms were assigned to the act, such as ethnic cleansing, paternalism, and even genocide.

Andrew Jackson's reputation was highly unquestionable at this point. While most of them criticized his act, some historians still admired his good leadership. For instance, Arthur Schlesinger, Jr., a famous historian, would praise Jackson for his strong-headed leadership but ignore the question about the design and implementation of the Indian Removal Act. In addition, Francis Paul Prucha was another personality who praised Jackson's steady act of the removal of the Five Tribes in 1969. He claimed that Jackson was the only reason for their survival in the present times. Writers such as Paul R. Bartrop and Steven Leonard Jacobs claimed that Jackson's acts did not justify this move to be a 'genocide' or a 'cultural genocide.' On the contrary, Jackson did face some massive blows from writers like Michael Paul Rogin and Howard Zinn, where the latter called him an "exterminator of Indians."

In 1987, the United States Congress declared and marked the Trail of Tears as a National Historic Trail to commemorate the death and suffering of the Native Americans. Moreover, in 2009, the path was almost doubled in size as new routes were documented along with several dispersion sites. According to the Omnibus Public Lands Management Act in 2009, the routes measured approximately 5,045 miles or about 8,120 km, which covered around nine states, namely, Alabama, Arkansas, Georgia, Illinois, Kentucky, Missouri, North Carolina, Oklahoma, and Tennessee.

So, what happened to the Native Americans following the horrendous incident? What happened to them? Where are the descendants now?

Currently, there are more than 570 recognized tribes in the United States. The term 'American Indian' does not include the groups of Native Hawaiians and a few Alaskan Natives. The U.S. Census-defined the Native Americans as American Indians, which also involve Alaskan Natives. In 1924, the Indian Citizenship Act was ruled out that recognized the Native Americans as U.S. citizens. Many of these tribal people did not hold official citizenship, which changed after this bill was passed. In the past, the United States Constitution passed the 'Indians not taxed' category that did not permit the Indians to vote in federal and state elections. However, with the passing of the Indian Citizenship Act, they were permitted to vote in elections. Moreover, the Fourteenth Amendment protections were extended and offered people the 'subject to the jurisdiction.'

Even after this act was ruled out, some states kept on discriminating against most of the Native American voters and did not allow them to vote; this continued for several decades. Apart from the Bill of Rights that was ruled out by the Indian Civil Rights Act in 1968, these did not apply to the tribal governments, which was a cause of concern.

U.S. Citizenship and the Native Americans

In 1924, Representative Homer P. Snyder (R) of New York ruled out the Indian Citizenship Act of 1924, also known as the Snyder Act, which offered full U.S. citizenship to American Indians. With the establishment of this act, about 125,000 of 300,000 indigenous people living in the United States were subjected to citizenship. At that time, some of the Native Americans were already citizens by either joining the armed forces, turning to a full-fledged

American lifestyle, or by giving up their tribal identity. Even with the passing of this Act, there were certain limitations to obtaining citizenship (like being an indigenous person from outside the United States or being born before the effective date as mentioned in the Act).

The situation changed after the Nationality Act of 1940 was passed. It claimed that any person born in the U.S. would be granted citizenship (with exceptions like being a child of a foreign diplomat). However, some Native Americans did not gain full citizenship and related rights until 1948. Until 1938, there were still seven states that did not allow the Native Americans to cast votes. Since there was a constant banter between federal and state governments, the Native Americans could not fully benefit from the enforcement of the Act. The states produced three concrete reasons that did not allow the Indians to be eligible to vote, which were -

- The Native Americans were exempt from real estate taxes,
- They lived under guardianship, and
- They were still affiliated with their tribal roots.

In 1928, the Meriam Report (a study conducted to produce real problems of the Native Americans) claimed that the indigenous people suffered from extreme poverty, exclusion of rights, and constant cultural oppression. In 1934, the Indian Reorganization Act was formed, which vouched to give back the Native Americans a part of their lands. They were also provided additional healthcare and education benefits.

In general, for the Native Americans to obtain U.S. Citizenship, the following factors were mandatory:

1. Treaty provision (as with the Cherokee)
2. Registration and land allotment under the Dawes Act of February 8, 1887
3. Issuance of Patent in Fee simple
4. Adopting Habits of Civilized Life
5. Minor Children
6. Citizenship by Birth
7. Becoming Soldiers and Sailors in the U.S. Armed Forces
8. Marriage to a U.S. citizen

9. Special Act of Congress.

Source: https://en.m.wikipedia.org/wiki/Native_Americans_in_the_United_States

Rising Concerns

As mentioned in the previous chapter, some of the descendants of the Seminole tribe still exist in Florida and surrounding regions. As per the recent U.S. census, around 6.8 million descendants of the Native American race still thrive in the county, which makes two percent of the total U.S. population. Out of these, around twenty-two percent have access to or live on tribal land. However, these reservations still face some issues that are directed toward their health care, education, loss of cultural roots and language, violence against women, and loss of tribal land.

Native American people are facing several issues even today, in the 21st century.

Health Care

Compared to general U.S. citizens, Native Americans are still grappling with the issue of healthcare. According to the Indian Health Service

(IHS), the life expectancy of most Native Americans is 5.5 years less than an ordinary U.S. citizen. The IHS operates to provide and promote health care norms to over 573 recognized tribal groups. In reality, the IHS doesn't have enough funds to conduct full-fledged operations; this is causing an increasing threat to the lives and health of the Native Americans. There is a significant lack of pharmacies, hospitals, and doctor's offices in a few tribal regions. According to the U.S. Commission on Civil Rights (2003), the Indian Health Care Improvement Act doesn't entirely meet the health needs of the county and is lacking by a whopping forty percent.

Moreover, the natives are also more prone to other diseases such as diabetes mellitus, chronic liver disease, and even homicide and suicide. This is partly because of the constant pressure of adapting to the Western lifestyle, which doesn't truly suit their native habits. It also includes diseases such as tuberculosis, cancer, and many heart-related health issues. The Native Americans aren't the only ones suffering; the population comprising Alaska Natives are also facing recurring health issues.

According to the Center for Disease Control and Prevention (2003), the Native Americans majorly suffer from heart disease, which has also been the leading cause of health-related death among the group. According to the HHS Office of Minority Health (2010), around thirty-six percent of Native Americans are at risk of dying before the age of sixty-five as compared to around fifteen percent of Caucasians, given they are suffering from heart disease. This is mainly because of a lack of opulent healthcare service, poverty, poor quality of nutrition, and increased risk of diabetes, which is why most Native Americans fear to die at a young age.

According to Indian Health Disparities (2001), around 117 percent of Native Americans run the risk of dying from diabetes, around 500 percent from tuberculosis, and eighty-two percent from suicide. According to Native People for Cancer Control (2005), cancer rates and death related to cancer is also high among most of these tribes. Since the diseases are carried forward in generations, infant death rates are also high.

All this data displays a significant concern for the Native Americans' healthy future. They are not only deprived of their rights but also basic needs, such as healthcare. If this continues further, the already-diminished population of Native Americans will start becoming extinct, which is an alarming aspect among the natives today.

Education

Compared to the general U.S. students who hold a graduation rate of eighty percent, Native American students hold a comparatively low graduation rate of sixty-seven percent. The main reason behind this low score can be directed toward a sincere lack of resources. Most of the leaders or significant figures that visit relevant schools have just one thing to say, "We really need to fix this. The floors were found damaged, and the water heaters did not work."

Housing

Housing is another basic need that is and has been a growing concern for the Indians. The reservations aren't receiving adequate housing to date. The Indian Housing Authority's (IHAs) is a concerned Organization that is consistently looking into providing or searching housing facilities for the Indians. In current times, around 90,000 Indian families are either homeless or facing an acute housing crisis. The ones that are already seated in their own houses are facing other issues. For instance, thirty percent of Indian families are overcrowded and live in congested spaces. Moreover, fifty percent of families lack a connection to public sewers, making it unhygienic for them to live there.

According to the U.S. Commission on Civil Rights (2003), most of the Native American families do not have adequate housing facilities, and their current homes are considered to be substandard. Most of the families are enlisted in the tribal housing waiting list, which often takes more than three years. Even if you are eligible for a house, you might possibly encounter overcrowding due to a lack of adequate spaces. Many tribal families live with two or three generations in a small space. A typical tribal housing comprises two bedrooms, inadequate plumbing, plausible lack of cooling and heating services, and kitchen.

Additional concerns are the lack of utilities. For most general U.S. populations, utilities such as electricity, running water, and active telephone lines are a necessity. But for the Native American families, some of these utilities are still a luxury, which is quite disheartening. So, factors like a major lack of space, overcrowding, lack of healthcare facilities, and an overall substandard way of living pose a threat to their health and further deteriorate their living and health conditions. The remote and rural areas are at a higher risk as the houses in these regions aren't connected to sewers and are inaccessible to health care centers.

Employment

The main governing bodies that operate the employment factors and job opportunities for the Native American tribes are the Tribal and federal governments. The tribes face a severe lack of employment, either because of a lack of jobs or due to discrimination. In reality, the lack of economic opportunity has left four to eight out of ten native adults jobless. According to the BIA American Indian Population & Labor Force Report (2005), most of the employed natives earn less than or almost equal to poverty wages, which has caused a major poverty drift among the population.

According to the American Indians Census Facts (2008), around 28.2 percent of Native

Americans live below the poverty line, which is a shocking number. The primary source of income for these natives is either through jobs or social security. In some cases, individuals are provided disabilities or veteran's income. Now, according to the National Center for Education Statistics (2006), the disparity of the families living below the poverty line has massively increased, from thirty-eight percent to sixty-three percent.

Since the natives are still facing a lack of employment opportunities, most of the adults and parents leave their homes and move to other regions or states to find work and provide for their families. The kids are left with their grandparents, shifting the entire responsibility onto them to raise and feed the kids. Also, families gather all the resources they own and sell them to get money to raise their kids and to meet basic needs such as food, clothing, education, and paying bills.

Tribal Land

Even though their ancestors owned massive acres of land, most of the descendants today do not have access to their land. As mentioned in one of the previous chapters, the tribal land conflict can be dated back to the period when the European colonizers tried to conquer the lands of Indians. The issue still stands for the modern-day Indians. These tribes are held 'in trust' by the federal government. They are provided land to stay, but they cannot buy or sell it. It basically means that they do not have ownership over their land, and it is, in fact, owned by the government.

The ownership of tribal lands has always been a topic of a dispute over the years, mainly between the state and federal government and the tribal people. Also, the natural resources on and around the land spike an entirely different debate altogether. For example, the Navajo community has been facing water disputes with the government. The debate revolves around water rights and ownership; this is the reason why over forty percent of Navajo households lack a supply of clean running water.

Loss of Cultural Roots and Tribal Language

It is not entirely shocking to know that the Native Americans are facing a loss of their cultural roots and their language. Most of the tribal people now speak English, which has diminished the chances of learning their own language. The tribes are starting to realize this problem and are continually engaged in teaching their native language to their kids and other members of their tribe. This effort has increased multifold and has molded into teaching classes, mobile applications, and other similar resources to promote and teach their language. Some of the main tribes that are involved in this movement include the Cherokees, Arapahoes, and Muscogee (Creek) Nation.

They follow the path of the founding director of the National Museum of the American Indian, W. Richard West Jr. (who governs the Cheyenne and Arapaho Tribes of Oklahoma). He once said, "Language is central to cultural identity. It is the code containing the subtleties and secrets of cultural life." The tribes take great pride in their language and want to pass it on to their new generations for more decades to come. They believe that if their language is alive, they will retain their significant identity and keep proliferating in history.

Inequality and Violence Against Women

In the past, Native Americans were known for their respect for women's equality. However, as time passed, most of the Native American households are facing a serious issue of violence against women. For a long time now, this problem has been pervasive among most of the native tribes. The numbers are so high that four in five American Indian and Alaska Native women regularly face violence. One in two women has also undergone sexual violence, which seems adverse. A highly catastrophic incident involves the murder of Native American women, which is ten times more than a general U.S. resident.

Apart from native women, native children also face violence on a regular basis. The Indian Law Resource Center noted that these children undergo three times more PTSD as compared to general U.S. children. To combat this situation, the House of Representatives passed the Violence Against Women Reauthorization Act of 2019, which offers a widened access to legal tools and acts for violence against women that involve acts like physical abuse, stalking sexual assault, and domestic violence.

What is the United States government's contribution to the existing Indian descendants?

The Native American population already suffered drastically in the past, which still seems to be continuing for most of the tribes in today's society. Some of them still even face racial discrimination. A few young descendants also find it difficult to 'fit in' with the general American youth. These issues weren't adequately addressed in the past. But with the rising awareness and severe lack of equality, the government and aspiring leaders are looking into making the lives of Native Americans better.

Recently, the first Native American presidential forum was held in the country, which involved the participation of Democratic presidential candidates such as U.S. Senators Elizabeth Warren, Bernie Sanders, and Kamala Harris. These candidates had a lengthy conversation with tribal leaders to discuss and understand their conditions, healthcare, education, and address the issues related to violence against women and children. This move was highly appreciated by most of the natives. A member of the Ojibwe tribe, Elizabeth Day, said, "It's great to finally get a lot of acknowledgment that Native Americans still exist, are still very much a part of civic engagement, and not an erased people."

Conclusion

T he forced exile of the Native Americans and the advent of the term 'Trail of Tears' is plausibly one of the most heinous acts of force, power, and territory in the world. This forced act that led to the death, imprisonment, and relocation of the Native Americans is recognized as genocide in today's world. It not only changed their lifestyles but also resulted in a major wipe-out of their legacy and home roots.

Irrespective of their time on the American continent, Native Americans were and will always be a significant part of American history. Most uninformed people often segregate the tales of Native Americans when they speak about or consider American history. But you must know that these anecdotes related to the Native Americans aren't separate from America. These tales are an essential part of American history that shouldn't be forgotten. Before the white men settled in, America belonged to the Indians - a fact that is often ignored in current times. If the Removal Act wasn't implemented, it would still majorly belong to these people. Both the European and American forces shrunk the Indian Territory by a great margin.

Now that you have an overview of their entire history, you can understand the endless annihilations they went through. However, irrespective of the situation or the consequences, these tribes showed bravery and fought back. Whether it was the European colonization or the Indian Removal Act, most of these tribes resisted and refused to give up their rights and ancestral roots.

It is important to note that these facts and anecdotes come from historical writings that possibly show just one side of the story or a specific viewpoint.

As you can see currently, with the present-day descendants of the Native Americans, the descendants are still facing a rising issue of poor healthcare service, unemployment, lack of housing, education resources, and a heaving issue regarding the loss of language and cultural roots. The forced exile that their ancestors faced completely ruined their roots and rights. In the beginning, the rule of Europeans forced them to switch to other lands that weren't theirs. It also resulted in the killing of a massive Native American population. The already-diminished population was then further troubled by the American federal and some state governments and were forced to move to other regions. In a refusal attempt, more Native Americans were killed either by a massacre or through starvation. The ferocious move from their homeland to a strange region, as we now know as the Trail of Tears, is a massive imprint in the history of America.

Even though most of the Native American population is wiped out, their impressive architectural implications, cultural roots, and ancestral significance thrive to date. They were and will always be an essential part of American history for years to come.

Resources

https://eji.org/news/history-racial-injus-tice-forced-removal-native-americans/

https://www.khanacademy.org/humanities/us-his-tory/the-early-republic/age-of-jackson/a/indi-an-removal

https://www.nationalgeographic.org/thisday/may28/indian-removal-act/

https://www.youtube.com/watch?v=E2YidQrQuec

https://www.youtube.com/watch?v=T8Hd42J-tzs

https://en.m.wikipedia.org/wiki/Indian_removal

https://www.youtube.com/watch?v=TTYOQ05o-DOI

http://www.nativepartnership.org/site/Page-Server?pagename=naa_livingconditions

https://mom.com/impact/important-issues-that-affect-native-americans-today

https://www.youtube.com/watch?v=6E9WU9T-Grec

https://en.wikipedia.org/wiki/Trail_of_Tears

https://en.wikipedia.org/wiki/Indian_Citizenship_Act

http://www.americaslibrary.gov/jb/jazz/jb_jazz_citizens_3.html

https://en.m.wikipedia.org/wiki/Native_Americans_in_the_United_States

https://www.britannica.com/event/Trail-of-Tears